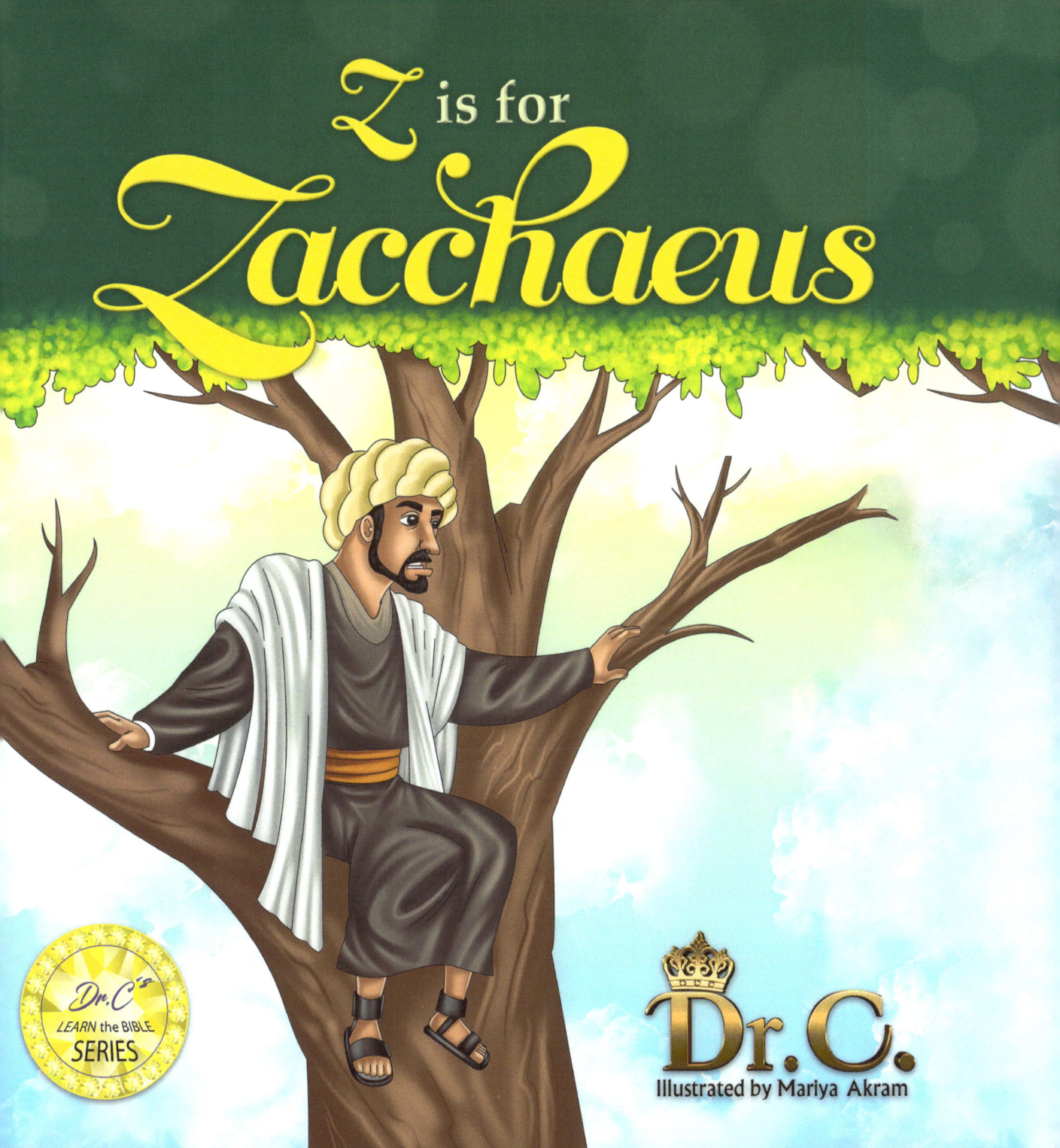

www.clfpublishing.org
909.315.3161

Copyright © 2022 by Cassundra White-Elliott.

All rights reserved. No portion of this book may be reproduced, stored in a retrieval system, or transmitted by any form or any means electronically, photocopied, recorded, or any other except for brief quotations in printed reviews, without the prior permission of the publisher.

Cover design by Senir Design. Contact info: info@senirdesign.com

Illustrations by Mariya Akram on Fivver.com.

ISBN #978-1-945102-86-8

Printed in the United States of America.

Dedicated

to all the students at

Excellence Academy

When Jesus lived on earth, He went from one town or city to another sharing the good news of how people could be saved from their sins. One of the towns He went to was Jericho. The people who lived there heard about His arrival, and many came out to see Him and to hear what He had to say.

In Jericho, there lived a man named Zacchaeus. Zacchaeus had heard that Jesus was coming to town. Like many other people, Zacchaeus wanted to hear what Jesus had to say. When Zacchaeus joined the crowd, he was too short to see Jesus. So, he decided to run ahead a bit and climb a tree. As Jesus was walking and talking, Zacchaeus knew eventually Jesus would pass by his way, and he would be able to get a good look at him.

To Zacchaeus' surprise, when Jesus reached the tree Zacchaeus was perched in, Jesus stopped and looked up. Jesus said, *"Zacchaeus, come down immediately. I must stay at your house today"* (Luke 19:5b, NIV). Zacchaeus was pleased and honored that Jesus wanted to go to his home, so he came down from the tree and took Jesus to his home.

Although Zacchaeus was excited about what was happening, many of the people who witnessed the entire situation were not. Tax collectors were not well liked by most people because they stole money from other people. And, the crowd of people could not understand why Jesus would want to go to someone's home who treated other people unkindly.

When Jesus and Zacchaeus arrived to Zacchaeus' home, Zacchaeus told Jesus he would give half of his possessions to the poor and he would repay anyone he had cheated four times as much as he had taken.
So even though the people of the town did not understand why Jesus could allow himself to be in the presence of a crooked tax collector, Jesus always has an open heart to everyone who wants to come to Him and stop doing what is wrong. Jesus gives all of us a chance to turn our lives around.

Instead of the people of the town disliking Zacchaeus, they could have shown compassion to him and given him an opportunity to do what was right. That's called having a heart of forgiveness. After Zacchaeus told Jesus what he was going to do, Jesus' heart was glad. He knew going to Zacchaeus' house was a great idea!

Can you be like Jesus and have a heart of compassion and be kind to others even when they are not kind to you? That is not an easy thing to do, but if you try, Jesus will show you how to be kind to others and share the love you have in your heart with them.

Color the picture on the next page, and while you are coloring, think about a time when you were not nice to someone. Did the person forgive you when you were mean?

If Jesus can be kind to us, we can be kind to others.

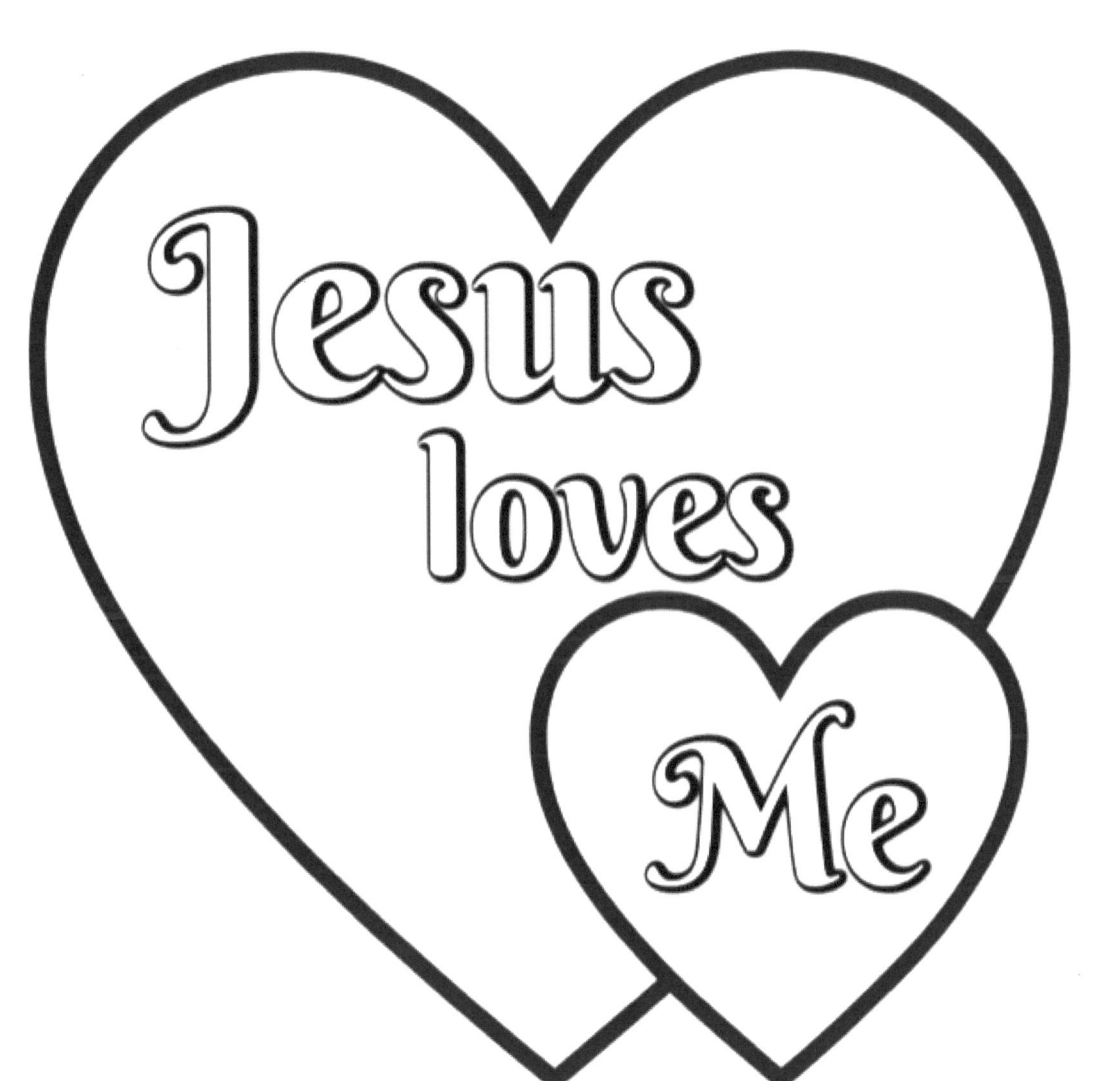

www.ingramcontent.com/pod-product-compliance
Lightning Source LLC
Chambersburg PA
CBHW041933160426
42813CB00103B/2902